HOLISTIC CHAKRA BALANCING

AND

THE POWER OF COLOR THERAPY

Martha Reed
Wings of Wisdom Publishing
Glendale, Arizona

HOLISTIC CHAKRA BALANCING

AND

THE POWER OF COLOR THERAPY

Published by:
Wings of Wisdom Publishing
Glendale, Arizona

ISBN 978-0991454501

Printed in the United States of America

CONTACT:
Martha Reed
20325 N 51st Avenue Suite 112
Glendale, AZ 85308
(623) 249 5888
Wings of Wisdom
insights@wingsofwisdompublishing.com

Published 2014
10 9 8 7 6 5 4 3 2 1

Advance Praise

A novice of the concepts of healing through natural or spiritual means, I wasn't sure what to expect from Dr. Reed's book. What I found was a lot of corresponding and pertinent information as the book goes directly and simply to the energy centers – explaining the process of balancing Chakras and providing basic explanations as to the effects various colors have on the body – particularly in tandem with Chakra Balancing. It's a good read for someone just beginning to delve into discovering these two modalities, but I believe readers with a more advanced understanding would still benefit from having this book in their library.

~T. R. Stearns, EdS

I just finished reading Dr. Reed's first book on Chakra balancing and its soul mate, color therapy. Since it is a new topic for me, I thought I would read a few pages and then come back later to finish; I just couldn't stop! The book, written in a terrific blend of theory, practice and an almost conversational tone, is a work that has totally convinced me of the merits of balancing Chakras and the role they play in our overall health. Adding in color therapy as part of the overall discovery of better health, I found myself identifying with many of the comments made, and made me eager to integrate the practices in my life. I certainly look forward to more similar work by this author.

~ **Anna Weber | Literary Strategist**

Foreword

I am honored to introduce this new work by my dear friend and ally Martha Reed. How can it get better than this?' Martha didn't just write about various alternative-healing modalities... she is sharing a lifetime of professional work using them. Healers use a combination of protocols to help their clients understand the underlying cause of their dis-ease, to release the energies that need to be released, and to realign their energy bodies. Chakra Balancing and the Power of Color Therapy is the result of Reed's years of passionate study, consistent research, and conscientious work with her clients. An insightful heart and mind have served Dr. Martha on her journey - these things are evident in the manner in which she shares her knowledge and expertise in working with using a holistic approach to life healing through Chakra Balancing and the power of Color Therapy. As a healer, Reed has long used a combination of modalities to help her clients understand the underlying cause of their dis-ease... and ultimately release available and necessary energies to realign their energy bodies. Readers will come to embrace the reality that, "When our chakras are balanced, our bodies experience natural healing, and overall good health is reinstated and experienced."

Dr. Martha does a stellar job of sharing wisdom, expertise and experience. It is an empowering book for those interested in alternative healing methods. It is an "easy" read, interesting and easy to apply for anyone new to the concept of tapping into their body's energy centers. Readers will quickly connect with "imagining colors" throughout specific areas of the body, to ultimately experience the kind of peace and calm that accompany the clearing of negative energy. It is definitely one of those, "It is too good to be true" concepts... until you experience it! Chakra Balancing and the Power of Color Therapy definitely helps readers begin that journey.

~ Greg S. Reid
Author | Filmmaker | Dad
www.BookGreg.com
www.333films.com

Dedication

I dedicate this book to the subtle nudge that encouraged me every day!

… and to Kristine Van Hook for her countless hours (although kicking and screaming) helping me with my research and dissertation along with Jeri Jo Anderson for believing in my dream and gifting me with a Color Therapy Light system, both of which were invaluable to bringing this book to fruition.

Table of Contents

Introduction

Thank you for investing in yourself and for sharing a journey with me to discovering the benefits of integrating Holistic Chakra Balancing and the Power of Color Therapy in your lives. Although the materials began as part of my own discovery as the foundation for my dissertation, they have become an integral part of my work and the message I share. The two topics, when combined, bring that discovery process and ultimate benefit to a broader audience. In order to retain the purity of my topics, the book is presented in two major sections, discussing first Holistic Chakra Balancing, followed by the Power of Color.

Is this book for you? It is if you want to feel good, balanced, relaxed... and generally whole and healthy. It is also for you if you like the idea of becoming a people magnet because you radiate positive energy. And... it is perfect if you feel like your life is just out of balance or you have that empty feeling of being sad and not understanding why.

SECTION I

| Holistic Chakra Balancing

Does Western Medicine Ignore the Elephant in the Room?

More people than ever before in the United States are dissatisfied with Western medicine and are feeling the need to do "something different" when it comes to improving their health and well-being. Many are understandably, growing increasingly frustrated with the notion that they need to "learn to live with chronic conditions" and the use of long-term or lifelong medications and medical therapies. The hope that chronic conditions can be reversed, or even cured, is lost to Western medicine in many cases. "It is estimated that about 125 million Americans have one or more chronic

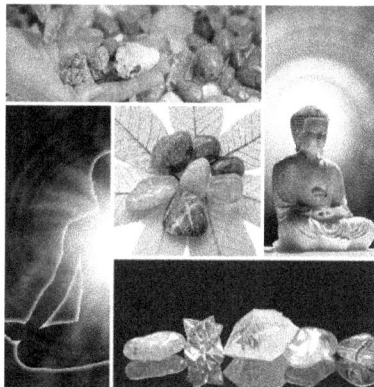

diseases, one half of whom have two or more chronic illnesses" (Geyman, 2007).

Western medicine, also called conventional or mainstream medicine, is defined as "Medicine as practiced by holders of M.D. (medical doctor) or D.O. (doctor of osteopathy) degrees and by their allied health professionals, such as physical therapists, psychologists, and registered nurses." (Medicinenet.com, 2009). It is practiced throughout the Western world (North America and Europe) and relies on scientific evidence to make decisions regarding client care and treatment. Western medicine does not deviate from the evidence at hand; therefore, medical treatment lacking scientific evidence is considered anecdotal, experimental, or alternative, and usually not recommended or practiced. Western medicine is also based on what is "known" to work based on scientific confirmation.

The Impact of the Affordable Care Act

There is a positive side to the Affordable Care Act – the possibility that alternative medicine could become more respected within the mainstream health care system. Unless… something in the fine print of the overly large document falls short due to unclear language or inadequate oversight. In fact, one clause of the law – Section 2706 – is being discussed by those practicing alternative medicine because of the language directing insurance companies "Shall not discriminate" against any health provider with a state-recognized license. Additional support appears to be coming from other sections of the law as well, addressing wellness, prevention and research.

It is no longer uncommon for healthcare providers without the usual medical background to manage myriad client doubts. I believe as we move forward, and embrace wholistic practices; it is nothing more than a matter of education and cultural change. In reality, according to the National Institutes of Health 2007 survey, approximately 4 in 10 adults in the U.S. currently rely on some form of alternative medicine.

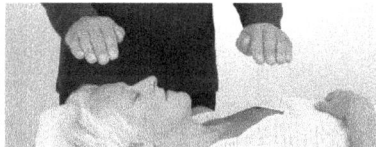

Clients want positive outcomes for good value; this is my hope for the future of medicine… the potential of our health care system taking an integrative approach of conventional or alternative healing.

In recent years, due to the skyrocketing health care costs for clients with chronic conditions, disease management has become the new 'big business' of the Western health care industry. It is estimated that "disease management industry revenues are likely to exceed $2.8 billion by 2010" (Leading Disease Management Organizations, 2008).

The focus of Western health care has turned to reducing costs, and therefore, managing diseases in our society has become far more important than finding the cure. Clients have become disillusioned by an overpriced health care system that is motivated solely by cost. There is no financial reward for healthy outcomes, and in fact, chronically ill clients are, by far, the primary consumers of the Western health care industry. "The care of chronic illness accounts for almost 75% of total health care expenditures each year. Just five chronic diseases—hypertension, heart disease, diabetes, asthma, and mood disorders—account for almost one half of US health care spending" (Geyman, 2007). As Geyman states, "...care instead of cure is the major goal."

Updating these statistics, according to the Center for Medicare and Medicaid Services data studied for 2012,

"In 2012 U.S. health care spending increased 3.7 percent to reach $2.8 trillion, or $8,915 per person, the fourth consecutive year of slow growth. The share of the economy devoted to health spending decreased from 17.3 percent in 2011 to 17.2 percent in 2012, as the Gross Domestic Product increased nearly one percentage point faster than health care spending at 4.6 percent.

To further explore where those funds were expended, updated information from 2012 was provided by the Centers for Disease Control and Prevention:

Percent of national health expenditures for hospital care: 31.4% (2010)

Percent of national health expenditures for nursing home care: 5.5% (2010)

Percent of national health expenditures for physician and clinical services: 19.9% (2010)

Percent of national health expenditures for prescription drugs: 10.0% (2010)

Long before the ongoing issues with the Affordable Health Care Act, employers began shifting their response to the rising health care costs by developing cultures of health within their companies. In an Aware article by Minnesota Life, the company addressed the trend of employers to challenge their staff to assume personal roles in health care by taking advantage of behavioral and lifestyle changes – to decrease medical spending, and achieve a better ROI on the costs being expended, by incorporating integrative holistic medicine into their health plans.

Furthermore, the idea of long-term or lifelong medications and routine follow-up physician visits doesn't sit well with many people nowadays, especially when it becomes so costly to maintain such a schedule. Many people can't keep up financially, leaving them in a position of feeling that they are victims of an unaffordable system; they often find themselves in the position of having to reject necessary treatments (which may leave them in a state of deteriorating health). Even if it were affordable, Western medicine offers clients little hope of getting off medications and recovering from conditions such as chronic pain, obesity, diabetes, mental disorders, and other chronic conditions such as fibromyalgia, chronic fatigue syndrome, and many others.

Many clients become unhealthily dependent upon medications that alleviate the symptoms, but never really fix the problems.

Are we, in the Western world, ignoring "the elephant in the room?" Disease prevention or cure is becoming a dinosaur concept, as we continue to get sicker and sicker, and require more and more "disease management." This is not to say that disease management does not have its proper place; in cases where disease has progressed unchecked, disease management may be the only option available. However, even in such cases, disease management does not have to be a lifelong, or even a long-term, sentence.

There is another way for resolving health issues, and it is found in energy medicine. Energy medicine relies upon ancient principles found in Eastern medicine, that go back thousands of years. Essentially, everything is energy and everything has the capacity to self-heal. Therefore, Eastern medicine involves working with energy to correct health issues. It is practiced throughout the Eastern world (Asia and Eastern Europe, which includes Russia, India, the Far East, Middle East, and Central Asia). Energy medicine is intuitive by design, based on unseen and immeasurable forces, which goes against the teachings of Western medicine.

HOLISTIC CHAKRA BALANCING

According to Eastern medicine, when the human energy fields become unbalanced, dis-ease in the physical body is more likely to occur, especially when energy remains unbalanced for long periods of time. Physical dis-ease is simply a manifestation of energy imbalances. Any correction in the human energy field leads to improved health and well-being.

In this book, I seek to share the understanding of energy medicine, the human subtle energy bodies, and Chakras, and to explore the effectiveness of holistic Chakra balancing in several clients using alternative holistic methods. It is my belief that holistic Chakra balancing can improve well-being on all levels: physical, emotional, spiritual, and mental. Getting our Chakras in balance (and maintaining consistent Chakra balance) is the key to improving health and eliminating (or avoiding) chronic conditions altogether. Energy medicine has the potential to transform Western health care. It doesn't have to be "one or the other" or "all or nothing." Energy medicine can be integrated into Western medical practices, as a way to improve the success rate of treatments and health outcomes.

An Overview of Energy Medicine

The following is an overview of energy medicine, the seven subtle energy bodies, the seven primary Chakras, the seven-year life cycles of human development that relate to each Chakra, and the various techniques used in holistic Chakra balancing.

Energy Medicine

C. Norman Shealy, M.D., founding president of the American Holistic Medical Association states, "Energy medicine is the future of all medicine." Dr. Mehmet Oz, professor of cardiac surgery at Columbia University and medical guest for Oprah Winfrey stated that: "We're beginning now to understand things that we know in our hearts are true, but we could never measure. As we get better at understanding how little we know about the body, we begin to realize that the next big frontier… in medicine is energy medicine. It's not the mechanistic part of the joints moving. It's not the chemistry of our body. It's understanding for the first time how energy influences how we feel."

To understand the foundation of this work, it is necessary to ask, "What is energy medicine?" According to Donna Eden, a pioneer in energy medicine, "Energy medicine recognizes energy as a vital, living, moving force that determines much about health and happiness. In energy medicine, energy is the medicine, and energy is also the client. You heal the body by activating its natural healing energies; you also heal the body by restoring energies that have become weak, disturbed, or out of balance. Energy medicine is both a complement to other approaches to medical care and a complete system for self-care and self-help. It can address physical illness and emotional or mental disorders, and can also promote high-level wellness and peak performance" (Eden, 2008).

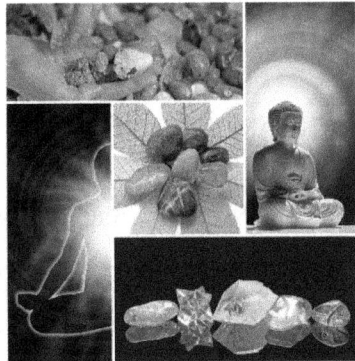

According to Eden, there are nine primary energy systems:

1) Meridians;

2) Chakras;

3) Aura;

4) Electrics;

5) Celtic Weave;

6) The Five Rhythms;

7) Triple Warmer;

8) Radiant Circuits; and

9) Basic Grid.

For the purposes of this study, I have focused on the aura and the Chakras.

The Human Biofield: Subtle Energy Bodies

Beyond the physical body, humans have a biofield, which is also referred to as an aura. The biofield (aura) is defined simply as the energy (luminous radiation) that surrounds a person's physical body. This biofield contains seven primary energy layers, called subtle energy bodies. These all exist as layers in the human biofield. Intuitives (those people who are able to perceive the "unseen" through a sixth sense) are sometimes able to perceive fields of color that surround the physical body.

Barbara Ann Brennan, a former research scientist for NASA and founder of the Barbara Brennan School of Healing, best describes subtle energy bodies in her book Hands of Light: A Guide to Healing Through the Human Energy Field. She is considered an authority in human energy fields and explains the subtle energy bodies in detail, which are outlined below. Subtle bodies follow the ROYGBIV color spectrum rays of light frequency, that is to say, Red, Orange, Yellow, Green, Blue, Indigo, and Violet. Each subtle energy body has its own set of seven Chakras.

Mundane Bodies

There are four mundane bodies, which are the densest and lowest subtle energy bodies.

Physical Body: This is the body that exists on the physical plane that we perceive through our five senses: touch, sight, smell, hearing, and taste.

First Layer – Etheric Body: The etheric body is just above the physical body, and it is the closest to the physical body. It is in the etheric body where alternative therapies such as homeopathy, Reiki, and energy work can occur (discussed in greater detail below). It appears as red.

Second Layer – Emotional Body: This body is just above the etheric body and it rules over basal emotions. All our human feelings exist in the emotional body, such as anger, fear, frustration, sadness, and happiness. It appears as orange.

Third Layer – Mental Body: Just above the emotional body is the mental body, and it contains all our thoughts and ideas. Habitual thoughts have a great impact on the physical body, whether negative or positive. Discipline of mind and purity of thought are very important, since thoughts become reality in the physical body. It appears as yellow.

Higher Consciousness Bodies

Understanding the concept of higher consciousness bodies follows the awareness of the four mundane bodies. These basically repeat the concepts (physical, emotional, mental) of the mundane bodies, but at higher levels of consciousness.

Fourth Layer – Etheric Template Body: This, the first body of higher consciousness, is affected by meditation. It is said to be the template upon which the physical body is created. This body disciplines the lower mundane bodies; it is also called the body of "higher will." Emotions, thoughts, and actions are brought under control in this body. It appears as green.

Fifth Layer – Celestial Body: This layer is the spiritual emotional body and is the body of unconditional love. It is in this body that we feel connected to the Source... to become One with God; when we realize that everything is and always is "love and light." It is the body of higher spiritual emotions. It appears as blue.

Sixth Layer - Ketheric or Causal Body: This is the mental level of the spiritual plane, and is the body of "higher concepts." The feeling of "knowing" comes from this body. It is where belief systems originate from a deep inner knowing. It appears as indigo.

Seventh Layer – Transpersonal or Cosmic Body: In this body, we move beyond the levels of incarnation; being more than just the body. It is the place of immortal consciousness. It appears as violet. (Brennan, 1988)

The Chakras

In addition to the seven subtle bodies, there are seven primary Chakras. Chakra comes from the Vedic Sanskrit word, which translates as "wheel." (Vedic Sanskrit is the oldest language of India, and was a precursor to classical Sanskrit.) In Eastern medicine, Chakras are whorls or vortices of energy located within the etheric body. In ancient literature, there are 88,000 reported Chakras. For the sake of clarity and simplicity, only the seven primary Chakras are discussed, which are the most well-known among holistic practitioners.

The Chakras start at the base of the spine and follow up the spine to the top of the head. They are listed in order from the base of the spine to the top:

Root Chakra

Sacral Chakra

Solar Plexus Chakra

Heart Chakra

Throat Chakra

Brow, or Third Eye Chakra

Crown Chakra

It is hypothesized that the endocrine glands are the physical manifestations of the seven primary Chakras (Judith, 1999). The Chakras occur within the energy bodies, whereas the glands occur on the physical realm, within the physical body. Chakras are simply different aspects of consciousness.

Any imbalance in consciousness plays out in the Chakras, and could lead to an imbalance in hormones secreted by the endocrine glands… the endocrine system regulating body functions through the productions of hormones. If any aspect of consciousness is out of balance for too long, physical disease can manifest. Below is a list (from densest to lightest) of the seven primary Chakras, their colors, and corresponding endocrine glands:

The heart Chakra lies in the middle of the Chakras. There are three Chakras above and three Chakras below the heart Chakra. The three lower Chakras deal with aspects of consciousness related to base human needs and emotions. The three upper Chakras deal with higher aspects of consciousness related to intellect and spirituality. The heart Chakra balances the Spirit with the flesh. The heart Chakra is the seat of unconditional love and divine grace. When hormones are imbalanced, specific Chakras therapies may be helpful to restore hormonal balance on a physical level.

Chakra Consciousness

Each Chakra holds specific life issues, or consciousness. Any dis-order or imbalance in consciousness will create hormone imbalances as well, thereby affecting the whole being. Below is a list of the Chakras and issues:

Root: Foundation, self-preservation, survival instincts and grounding.

Sacral: Emotions and sexuality.

Solar Plexus: Power and energy

Heart: Love, compassion, connecting mind and body.

Throat: Communication and self-expression

Third Eye: Intuition.

Crown: Wisdom, spiritual connection, bliss, awareness and consciousness.

Chakra Balancing and Seven-year Life Cycles

In the beginning of the 20th century, Rudolph Steiner, a turn-of-the-century Austrian artist and seer, first proposed the concept that there are seven-year life cycles that are associated with the seven primary Chakras. The characteristics of the Chakra stage we are in become the base theme of our lives during each seven-year period. In the middle of life, at age 50, we start processing at the root Chakra level again, but at a higher state of awareness (Mercier, 30). Knowledge of the significance and purpose of each Chakra and life cycle can help us understand our personal issues throughout life and how to deal with each more effectively.

Root

The first stage of life is birth to seven years of age. This stage of life is associated with the root Chakra. During this time period, the infant can only think of himself and his own basic needs. This is a time of defining human base needs. The root Chakra brings up issues of survival, the right to exist, and to stand up for oneself (to be rooted into the earth and to hold a rightful place). According to Ambika Wauters, R.S. Hom, UK, expert in holistic Chakra balancing and director of the Institute of Life Energy Life Medicine, each human Chakra resonates with a specific right of being.

"The Root Chakra, located at the base of the spine, has a right to the life we say we want. It helps us become anchored in the earth forces that control cycles and rhythms and helps us move from a place of belonging and connection. It helps us to receive what is rightfully ours to experience in a way that allows us to assimilate what is nutritious and eliminate what is harmful. This occurs on all levels of being. When we do not possess a sense of this 'right to our own life,' then we lose our grounding, both psychologically and energetically, and lack confidence and authority about who we are and where we belong" (Wauters, 2009).

Any trauma occurring during this time period can result in feelings of insecurity, being ungrounded, and not belonging. Essentially, a person's foundation can become shaky if any type of trauma occurs or if base needs are unmet and unfulfilled during this time.

(Note: Between each stage, there is some degree of overlap in the transition year, i.e., 0-7, 7-14, 14-28, etc.)

Sacral

Between ages 7 and 14, personal values begin to emerge. During this time period, the child becomes aware of his or her differences. Likes, dislikes, and strong opinions are established during this time. This time period is associated with the sacral Chakra, which deals with social and personal intimacy, sexuality, and reproduction. Any imbalances or trauma during this time period can lead to emotional problems, relationship difficulties, and sexual dysfunction.

According to Wauters, "The right of the Sacral Chakra, which is located below the navel in the area of the pelvis, is our right to pleasure and abundance. When we deny ourselves ease and pleasure, abundance, and prosperity, we operate in a paradigm of lack and limitation. Whether we experience guilt or a sense of unworthiness we are not claiming our right to that which matches the abundance and creativity of the universe."

Childhood issues at this time can affect abundance and prosperity later in life, in all aspects, such as lacking relationships, isolation, lack of wealth and money, and so forth.

21

Solar Plexus

This time period – from 14 to 21 – includes the onset of puberty, and a desire to break away from parents and become an individual. This stage is associated with the solar plexus Chakra, which relates to personal power. Essentially, during this time you are entering your own personal power. According to Wauters, "The right of the Solar Plexus Chakra, located below the sternum, in the area of the stomach, is the right to our own power. This means that we know we are worthy of what we say we want, and we have sufficient self esteem to generate confidence and personal power."

Issues occurring during this stage of life can affect feelings of personal power later in life, and a person may have problems with powerlessness.

Heart

Between 21 and 28 years of age, commitment becomes important, either to a career or a person. Marriage and starting a family primarily occur during this stage of development, associated with the heart Chakra. The heart Chakra deals with the right to love, forgiveness, and compassion. According to Wauters, "The right of the Heart Chakra is the right to give and receive love. Many people only experience love as a giving out without cultivating the capacity to receive. When we allow love to enter into our lives we calm the heart and stabilize our emotions."

Issues during this time period may cause problems with loving others, self-love, and self-acceptance.

Throat

Between 28 and 35 years of age, creativity is strong and maturation takes place. This is a time for taking responsibility for creation. There is awareness that life is a manifestation of choices made in the past. This time is associated with the throat Chakra, which deals with the right to speak, express oneself, and the ability to trust. According to Wauters, "The right of the Throat Chakra is our right to self expression. When we express our truth, both our personal truth and the higher truth of God we open a channel for healing to happen in our life. Suppressing self expression creates tension and pathology."

Any issues during this period of life could lead to not being able to voice opinion, not being heard, not being able to defend opinion, and overall trouble with communication of personal needs.

Third Eye

Between 35 and 42 years of age is the time period for becoming an expert, and for fine-tuning life. It is associated with the third eye, which deals with intuition, insights, developing psychic abilities, and releasing hidden and repressed negative thoughts. According to Wauters, "The right of the Brow Chakra is our right to our own thoughts. Freedom to think intuitively is essential for a strong spirit. Discernment, knowledge, intuition, and imagination foster wisdom from which we make sense of the pain, loss, separation, and traumas of our life."

Imbalances during this time period may cause a disconnection with Spirit, blocked intuition, and closed-off psychic abilities.

Crown

The Crown Chakra period occurs between the ages of 42 to 49. The end of the first seven life cycles at the age of 49 signifies the middle of life, and it is during this cycle that the "midlife crisis" usually occurs. After the midlife crisis, life turns inward toward spiritual development and fulfillment before death.

This is a major turning point in life, and the Crown Chakra governs it. The Crown Chakra is all about connecting with higher consciousness, with becoming connected to the higher self and higher levels of consciousness, and connecting to the etheric body. A time for integrating consciousness with super-consciousness this is a time when dreams may come true, because there is a connection with super-consciousness and manifesting it in the physical realm. According to Wauters, "The right of the Crown Chakra is the right to our indelible connection with the Creator. Without a sense of this eternal connection, we give over our spiritual will to others to define what and who we are as spirit."

During this stage, there is a lack of concern of what other people think. There is a strong sense at this point, of "who I am" and no willingness to compromise within relationships, meaning that the person will not negotiate his or her belief system for others.

Once this seven-year life cycle is completed, then the full cycle repeats itself at an enlightened or higher spiritual level, starting with the root, and moving up to the crown once again.

Root (Repeat Begins)

Between the ages of 49 and 56, the Chakra cycle begins anew, at a higher level of consciousness. Issues and imbalances in the Root Chakra are once again addressed and explored at this time. The revealing question to ask those in this stage of existence, "Do you feel like you are comfortable and secure at this point in life?"

This is a stage of transformation, where you realize that you have indeed created your own reality. You become aware that everything you have done throughout your life has gotten you to "this point." There is a greater need for discernment and not jumping into things without careful evaluation. Unfortunately, physical illnesses tend to manifest at this time.

Sacral

Between the ages of 56 and 63, the issues of the Sacral Chakra are re-addressed, in particular abundance and prosperity. Intimacy and sexuality exist at a higher spiritual level, and relationships become much deeper and more spiritually based.

Solar Plexus

Since the solar plexus deals with issues of power, between the ages of 63 and 70, there is a surrendering of the ego power. Power becomes more a spiritual experience, rather than an ego experience. Power becomes much of an experience of going within, instead of trying to control the external environment (people and circumstances).

Heart

Between 70 and 77 years of age, the wise person who has lived to this point will feel more at peace than ever before, and will become more reflective, knowing that death may only be a few years away. Pleasure comes from the simple things, materialism becomes less of a priority, and just "being" becomes more of an everyday occurrence. This is the time for heart-centered spiritual action, and for enjoying life at a deeper level of awareness and with greater consciousness.

Throat

Between the ages of 77 and 84 years of age, there is a reawakening of self-expression. No longer is there a need to care about what other people think about "what you have to say." It is during this time that you can become very vocal and outspoken.

Third Eye and Crown

Between 84 and 91 years of age and beyond (if life expectancy continues beyond the human average), the parent requires the care of the child, once again becoming dependent upon another for basal needs, and completing "the circle of life." This becomes the sense of birth into "the unknown" of death.

Holistic Chakra Balancing Techniques

Holistic Chakra Balancing techniques are used to balance the Chakras at any given point in life. By understanding the subtle energy bodies, the Chakras, and seven-year life cycles, it becomes easier to identify the underlying causes of Chakra imbalances and disease. There are many tools and techniques available to balance the Chakras. The primary techniques are reviewed below: Color, crystal, sound, aromatherapy, homeopathy, and hypnotherapy. The chart below lists the Chakra, its color, its musical note, and a crystal recommendation for each. Note that crystal recommendations are based on color. For instance, red jasper is for the red Root Chakra.

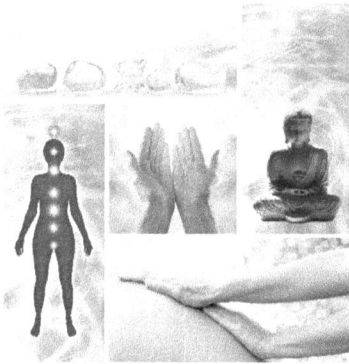

Crown

White or violet

Music Note B

Amethyst, Clear quartz

Third Eye

Indigo

Music Note A

Lapis, Lazuli, Azurite, Sugilite

Throat

Blue

Music Note G

Sodalite, Blue Calcite, Blue Kyanite, Angelite, Blue Turquoise

Heart

Green or Pink

Music Note F

Green Aventurine, Malachite, Jade, Green Calcite, Rose Quartz, Pink Tourmaline

Solar Plexus

Yellow

Music Note E

Citrine, Yellow Jasper, Golden Calcite

Naval/Sacral

Orange

Music Note D

Orange Calcite and Carnelian

Base/Root

Red

Music Note C

Red Jasper and Garnet

Color Therapy

Color therapy is also called Chroma therapy and it involves bringing in color as a way to "feed the Chakras." Color therapy is also referenced as vibrational medicine, which according to the historical principles of vibrational medicine... supports that everything has a pulse inside of it, or "hums" to a specific vibration. Remedies that vibrate at specific frequencies are used to balance energy. Examples of vibrational medicine include color, sound, crystals, plants (flower essences), and herbs.

Colors are a form of electromagnetic energy. Each color resonates at a particular vibration, just as each human energy center, or Chakra, resonates at a certain vibration (Koltsche,

1994). Putting a red crystal in your pocket or in a medicine pouch, wearing a red garment, and eating red foods are all ways to balance Chakras with a specific color.

Colors can bring out strong physical, emotional, mental, and spiritual reactions giving rise for color therapy to help balance aspects of consciousness. For example, someone who is having trouble with survival issues or belonging can use the color red to balance higher levels of consciousness that are affected. Many times, a strong negative or positive reaction to a specific color can signal an imbalance in a specific Chakra. For example, someone who is repelled by green might be having underlying trouble with self-love, acceptance, and relationships.

If someone is focused too much on the color green, it may mean that there is an overstimulation of the Chakra, and that there may be an addiction to love and unhealthy relationships. Simply reflecting these as examples, it is important to note that color experiences are very unique to the individual.

Crystal Therapy

Crystal therapy is sometimes also referred to as "laying on of stones." It involves using crystals to balance energy.

Each crystal has unique properties with specific vibrations. The crystals are placed on the person's Chakras while he or she is lying down. Crystals can also be held during meditations, or worn in a medicine pouch. They can be programmed and cleared to release any negative energies and to promote balancing, clearing, and releasing of the major Chakras.

Sound Therapy

Each Chakra resonates to a specific musical note (as outlined in the previous table). Chakra imbalances may also be detected and balanced by using musical instruments. Aversion or attraction to a particular musical note may indicate an imbalance or harmony in the corresponding Chakra, respectively, depending on the person's reaction. Music therapy is a powerful tool that can be used to restore Chakra balance. Jonathan Goldman, a Grammy nominee, is the modern-day authority and pioneer in sound therapy for Chakra balance. Sound therapy is also part of vibrational medicine, where different sound frequencies (vibrations) have the ability to accelerate healing (Goldman, 2008). For example, playing the "C" note will help balance the root Chakra; playing the "D" note will help facilitate sacral Chakra balance, and so forth.

There are many different types of instruments that can be used. Common instruments that are used in music therapy include: therapeutic drumming, tuning forks, voice (chants, mantras, songs), and multimedia (audio CDs, DVDs). Quartz crystal bowls or Tibetan singing bowls are often used, because they create the sustained musical vibrations needed for Chakra balancing. The singing bowls are produced in such a way that striking the sides, or running a wooden stick around the rims, produces the healing sounds needed for Chakra balancing.

Hypnotherapy

In the case of holistic Chakra balancing, hypnotherapy can be used to take the client through a regression to the time period(s) where the Chakras became imbalanced in the first place – not just in this lifetime, but also in past lifetimes (many people believe that we are reincarnated; therefore, in the current lifetime, we are the sum of all our incarnations). Regressing to past-life and current-life traumas and finding the cause(s) of the imbalances can help clear and balance the particular Chakra being affected. Hypnotherapy involves facilitating access to a person's subconscious through hypnosis.

Using the seven-year life cycles as a reference can also be very helpful. For example, if an infant is mistreated some time between birth and seven years of age, hypnotherapy can help regress the client to the root cause of insecurity and instability. Hypnotherapy can help erase an old painful memory and replace it with a new memory of peace and happiness. It can also replace negative thought patterns with positive thought patterns.

Homeopathy

The concept that "like cures like" was first mentioned by Hippocrates, who is said to be the "ancient founder of medicine." German physician Samuel Hahnemann (1755-1843) later developed the field of homeopathy (Waters, 2007).

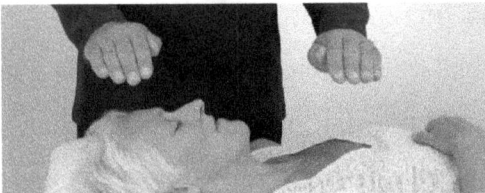

The practice is based on the premise that every person has a life force, or what Oriental medicine refers to as chi. Chi is translated as "energy flow." It is the concept that energy sustains life. Without energy, there can be no life. When chi (energy flow) is disrupted, health problems occur.

The word homeopathy comes from the Greek homeo, which means similar, and pathos, which means disease. Homeopathy involves providing minute doses of substances that would normally invoke symptoms when given in larger doses, in order to invoke the body's self-healing response. The idea is that a substance that causes illness can also cure it. For instance, while the red onion will cause the eyes to become red, burning, and irritated, it will also cause the eyes to tear up and the nose to run. The essence of the red onion acts as an aid to the body's natural defense system, triggering it to clear. Homeopathy is used in holistic Chakra balancing in order to invoke the self-healing response as a way to balance the Chakras.

During my initial exposure to homeopathy, I was caught by the reality there is very little energy theory compared to the coverage of Ayurvedic or Chinese medicine – although the chakra system of energy is found in the oldest systems of medicine. As a practitioner, once you understand a remedy's energetic essence, symptoms become more predictable and the path to healing makes sense.

Fine-tuning my skills requires me to embrace new tools having the potential to increase my knowledge – that I might remain in the profession of healing rather than fall into upholding "tradition" as is more prevalent with modern medicine. At the end of the day… what remains of utmost importance is returning a client to good health and a healthy lifestyle. I am reminded of Edgar Cayce, reminding us that healing of the physical without the change in the mental and spiritual aspects brings little real help to the individual in the end'. In essence, working with clients from a homeopathic therapy, I am asking them to create their own level of energy, trusting my unique gifts to provide the doorway to integrating this modality, not only that they might realize healing, but ever-deepening levels of perception.

Aromatherapy

Aromatherapy can also be used to stimulate the Chakra balancing process. Aromatherapy involves the use of plant-derived essential oils to induce healing. Essential oils are the pure essence of a plant, and they are selected according to a specific medicinal need. They can be applied on the skin or inhaled. Essential oils can be placed in diffusers and inhaled while the client is participating in other holistic treatments, such as hypnotherapy, sound, and/or color therapy, for example. In many cases, smells can trigger past-life and current life issues that can come up to the surface for clearing.

Aromatherapy can also integrate the body with nature, producing a deep state of relaxation. As Kurt Schnaubelt, Ph.D., points out in his book Advanced Aromatherapy: The Science of Essential Oils, "For those stressed by civilization, aromatherapy offers nature in a bottle. Nature interacting with humans in many more ways than are possible with conventional products." In 1937, René-Maurice Gattefossé, a French chemist, wrote a book called Aromathérapie: Les Huiles essentielles hormones végétales, which was subsequently translated into English and titled Gattefossé's Aromatherapy. He began his work in aromatherapy when he accidently burned his arm and put it in a large container of lavender essential oil to try to stop the burn. He noticed that the burn healed rapidly without any scars.

The following represents the seven primary Chakras and a recommendation of essential oils that may be helpful in balancing them (TheHealingMassage.com, 2009):

Root: Myrrh, Patchouli, Vetiver, Rosewood, Thyme, Balsam de Peru

Sacral: Sandalwood, Clary Sage, Cardamom, Fennel, Bergamot

Solar Plexus: Juniper, Cedar wood, Hyssop, Marjoram, Coriander

Heart: Rose Maroc, Bergamot, Melissa, Ylang Ylang, Geranium, Jasmine, Lavender, Mandarin, Tangerine

Throat: Chamomile, Linden Blossom, Cypress, Petit grain, Basil, Peppermint, Hyssop, Rosemary, Rosewood

Third Eye: Rosemary, Juniper, Hyacinth, Lemon, Pine, Angelica Seed, and Geranium

Crown: Neroli, Rose, Frankincense, Lavender

It is important to note that these are suggestions, and they are provided only as examples. Essential oils should be customized to the individual's circumstances and health needs.

| The Road to Discovery

Disease or dis-ease in life does not have to define you, and while the concept holds merit, to a certain extent anything that impacts our health ultimately changes the way we embrace life. Knowing you can no longer accomplish the things in life to which you had held such passion, there is equal passion, then to manage your health in such a manner that you know no limitations; including alternative methodologies, such as Holistic Chakra Balancing and Color Therapy.

Holistic Chakra balancing therapy consists of balancing the seven primary Chakras. Preparing to publish this book, I worked with numerous clients and used many of the above-mentioned combinations of holistic Chakra balancing techniques, including color, aromatherapy, sound, crystal, homeopathy, and hypnotherapy, which were deemed best suited for the client's specific needs.

The holistic Chakra balancing therapy is initiated by performing a full intake evaluation to assess which Chakras were imbalanced. When possible, it is important to balance the Chakras from lowest to highest (from the root to the crown). Since each seven-year life cycle is associated with a Chakra, the holistic Chakra balancing therapy implemented focused on resolving any trauma that occurred during a particular seven-year life cycle in order to balance the corresponding Chakra. For example, therapy focused on clearing old patterns, traumas, and negative emotional associations that occurred during the first seven years of life that disrupted root Chakra balance, and so on.

Results were recorded in the following four case studies. Names have been changed in order to protect client confidentiality.

Sally:
Holistic Chakra Balancing Therapy

Sally presented as a 40-year old client who wanted to start a detox program. A detox program is a rapid method of clearing out toxins in the physical body through a variety of ways: food elimination and re-introduction, supplements, hydration and sweating, and colon hydrotherapy, just to name a few. Sally, in her impatience, wanted to "get rid of all the junk fast!" including excess, unwanted weight. She was also beginning to manifest physical symptoms, suffering from insomnia, weight gain, skin rashes, constipation, and heavy bleeding during menstruation. Sally also had fibroids and ovarian cysts and we discovered many of her physical problems were due to hormonal imbalances, unhealthy diet, not drinking enough water (hydration), and lack of exercise.

In the initial evaluation interview, it appeared on the surface that Sally merely wanted to overcome bad habits. However, in speaking with her, Sally expressed that she was having trouble even keeping a stable home. She had faced eviction from her apartment and was living with her mother for a brief period, while finding another place to live. Sally was not happy in the new rental property that she found for herself and was trying to overcome the anxiety and fear of being in this new home. All of these issues were preventing her from starting a new diet and a detox program.

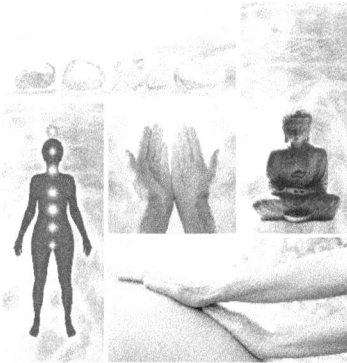

HOLISTIC CHAKRA BALANCING

We initiated Sally's holistic Chakra balancing therapy by feeding the root Chakra, where her unstable feeling about home created an imbalance. Sally was instructed to eat red foods, to carry red jasper, to wear red clothing, and to do a grounding meditation outside sitting on the grass to connect her root Chakra to the earth.

During the second week of following these recommendations, Sally's anxiety and repressed experiences started coming to the surface. During the next session, I walked Sally through a hypnotherapy session where she was able to go back to her childhood. Sally was able to make the connection that when she was 9, and again when she was 14, her family had to leave their home, only taking what they could fit in suitcases. Sally associated the loss of the home and all the belongings with an extreme sense of anxiety, which led to repeatedly recreating instability to avoid the feeling of "losing it all" again.

Instability and insecurity had become a chronic condition. If she didn't have a home... she wouldn't feel the pain. By finally acknowledging the feeling associated with the experience, Sally was able to overcome her feelings of anxiety associated with having a stable home. We were able to begin creating new memories associated with moving and being in a new home. The root Chakra was becoming more balanced.

Homeopathic remedies were also administered during several sessions, once for insomnia, and another time for head and ear congestion. The homeopathic remedies helped to invoke Sally's self-healing response in order to help clear the Chakras more effectively. While working on the root Chakra imbalances, Sally started a detoxification program that included shakes and supplements. As she began resolving her root Chakra issues, Sally's eating habits began to change. Naturally, in a matter of weeks, she had reduced her caloric intake and was eating less sugary foods, and also having less anxiety. Sally soon realized that she was stuffing anxiety with food. When anxiety about the home environment came to the surface, she found herself grabbing for sugary foods and drinks.

Once the connection was made between the root Chakra imbalance and the food, Sally was able to feel more at ease. Once the root Chakra was stabilized, the Chakra balancing therapy then continued to the second sacral Chakra, wherein Sally was instructed to wear orange, eat orange foods, and the like. The sacral Chakra deals with sexuality and emotions, so we explored these issues with her in detail using hypnotherapy as an aid for uncovering blocks. As each lower Chakra balanced, the upper Chakras began to balance as well.

According to the seven-year life cycles, at age 40 Sally was revisiting issues of her Third Eye, which deals with intuition and psychic ability. Since the root Chakra was not clear at the time, her Third Eye was also blocked. By clearing the root Chakra, Sally was able to open herself up to receiving intuitive messages from Spirit, and to gain better insight about solving her own challenges. During the sessions, she was given an Indigo color remedy to help balance the Third Eye.

By the time Sally finished her Chakra balancing therapy, she had made great progress in many aspects of her diet, emotional stability, and intuition. Her physical symptoms improved and she was sleeping better. She followed through on colon hydrotherapy and using an elimination diet to resolve underlying food allergies and leaky gut syndrome. Many of the physical imbalances were a result of not feeling stable (root) and blocked intuition (third eye).

Gypsy Rose:
Learning to Trust Your Gut

One particular client came to my practice with complaints of stomach issues that had begun as a small child. Gypsy Rose's parents were splitting up and her father was an abusive alcoholic. Eating dinner with the family involved conflict and strife, so these feelings became associated with not being able to eat and hold food down. After a visit to a physician, Gypsy Rose was told she had a nervous stomach and would suffer with it for the rest of her life and would need lifelong medication to ease her chronically nervous stomach. Her mother and father had different opinions about the matter: her father thought she should take the medication; however, her mother had the foresight to know that the mind is a powerful healing tool, and she worked with Gypsy Rose to overcome many of the fears associated with her inability to eat and her nervous stomach.

While working with Gypsy Rose, I realized that these stomach problems were related to imbalances in her sacral and solar plexus Chakras. One of the big clues to her Chakra imbalances was her hatred for the colors orange and yellow. Gypsy Rose's negative association to these colors led me to the conclusion that these two centers were imbalanced due to a lack of "feeding" them. Gypsy Rose literally had no orange or yellow in her daily life! Color therapy was used to help release past issues and balance these Chakras. As her practitioner, I started first with the sacral orange Chakra, since working from "the bottom up" has a positive effect on the upper Chakras. By working in the sacral Chakra first, the solar plexus Chakra started to become more balanced. I started her on an orange color therapy. I asked her to wear or hold the color orange every day in some fashion, by wearing orange clothing and undergarments; carrying orange rocks or crystals; and consuming orange foods. When she was comfortable, we went to the color yellow, and I asked her to do the same thing. I suggested she do the same schedule with yellow as she did for orange. It took about two months, but it completely shifted the imbalances. Orange and yellow are now two of Gypsy Rose's favorite colors, but more importantly, her stomach issues have been greatly relieved. On occasion, her stomach still feels discomfort, but she has learned to use it as a "radar," telling her that something is not right and needs to be resolved. The phrase "Trust your gut" now has a new meaning for her.

Betty:
Learning to Attach to Physical Reality

My client Betty complained of having trouble with "a detached feeling." She felt that she would leave her body and be out of control, almost feeling as if her body was being taken over by someone else. Once, when driving to work, she felt a detached feeling and could actually see herself driving the car. She had also been steadily gaining weight, feeling toxic, sluggish, and had no desire to take care of her personal daily responsibilities. Betty had been actively pursuing her psychic abilities and was spending a lot of time with crystals, using them to clear a lot of past karma and past-life issues through meditation, dowsing by herself, and with the help of other healers. Past and present wounds in this current lifetime

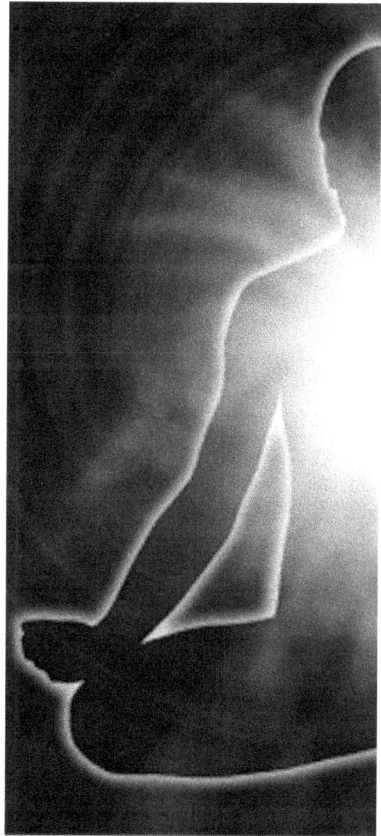

included interacting with a dominating father, a condemning mother, a verbally abusive brother, and having painful love affairs.

While working with Betty, I discovered she was detaching herself intentionally and unintentionally from life to avoid pain and had most likely followed this behavior throughout her life without realizing it. Past hurts and pains with her parents and siblings created a root Chakra imbalance, and abusive behaviors by family members created further imbalances in the sacral and solar plexus Chakras. All these painful relationships created heart and throat Chakra wounds as well... it was no wonder Betty was over-stimulating her third eye and Crown Chakra by seeking a connection with spirit as an ultimate escape from having to "feel" any of the basal emotions of the lower Chakras.

This detached feeling was actually an escape, so she would not have to feel anything. The weight gain Betty experienced during this time was her physical body's attempt to ground her and offer protection to the other energy centers. She was having a tug of war, so to speak. The more she mentally shifted into a spiritual connection, the more determined her body was to bring her back to physical reality. While she was "away" and not paying attention to her physical vehicle, she was creating physical damage by eating poorly and drinking unhealthily, which in turn caused a toxic body. This toxic overload contributed to her avoiding basic self-care, because she was not actively involved in her physical life.

I recommended Betty undergo a whole body detox program designed to rid the body of the toxins and eliminate any unknown food allergies that might be contributing to the imbalance as well. I also outlined a walking program for her: walking 30 minutes a day, with the first 10 minutes barefoot in the grass. I also instructed her to write down everything that moved around her during her walks: the birds, blades of grass, leaves, etc. Betty was asked to notice if anything moved under her feet. The next 20 minutes of walking (or more, if she could) would be around the neighborhood looking for "a miracle to appear" in the form of some small awareness with her outside environment. If she began to stray too much (daydreaming), Betty was instructed to count the cars and describe to herself what the drivers looked like and to remember the license plates as ways to focus her attention on her physical surroundings.

Betty was also given a checklist of body parts, and throughout the day, I instructed her to "check into her body" and write down how each individual part was feeling at that very moment. These exercises were created to bring her back into her body. She was also asked not to meditate for more than 15 minutes a day and instructed that the only crystals she could work with were red jasper, quartz crystal, and bloodstone. These stones resonate with the root Chakra, the color red, and help with clearing during detox programs.

It took more than one try to get through the detox, and Betty only did the walking exercise on occasion. The resistance to carrying out my recommendations indicated yet another escape tactic. Although she saw drastic improvement on the detox program, Betty was unable to continue with her new lifestyle; she was still attempting to master being physically present. Due to her ongoing resistance, I decided to try hypnotherapy combined with color therapy. Hypnosis was also used for past regression.

I brought Betty back to a time when she felt safe and then revisited times she felt unsafe or hurt. The painful times were revisited through new eyes, and we worked on rewriting the story in her memory, so that she could experience happy, peaceful outcomes, instead of painful ones. I recommended a color remedy of magenta, which is a combination of green for healing, red for safety, and violet for spiritual insight. This combination worked wonderfully; it helped Betty work through her past hurts with ease and grace, so that she could reduce the tendency to detach from physical reality and continue on her journey.

Martha Reed:
Walking the Talk

I had been experiencing chronic dietary issues, and my first attempt to find a connection between a toxic body and spiritual block was on myself (as a holistic practitioner). I had read a lot about the mind-body connection, and how what we eat has a direct connection to what we ultimately become. However, it must not have sunk in on every level… the after-holiday blues had set in, I had gained six pounds and my weight was on the rise. I was wondering why, with all I know about holistic health care, I consumed certain foods and beverages. I would then "beat myself up" about eating these items while "knowing better." Did I not have a better relationship with myself than that? The answer was, "Apparently not!" Hence, my own case study began.

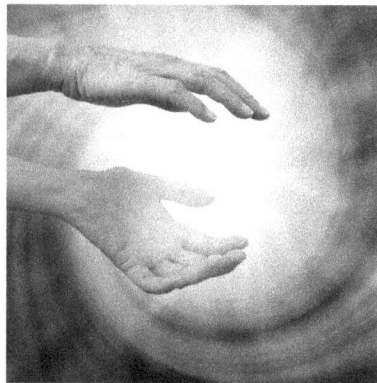

HOLISTIC CHAKRA BALANCING

I tried to cut out sweets first, failed miserably, and only craved them more. The more I tried and self-sabotaged, the worse I felt. The worse I felt, the less I did of the things I needed to do to feel better... like meditation, angel card readings, and exercise. Eating for health (and not taste) was once again a thing of the past, or at least not on my current schedule of things to do. I felt heavy, depressed, self-conscious, and wanted to retract into a shell like a hermit crab. I knew I had to do something to stop this snowball that was rolling downhill and picking up speed!

Detox! I thought, "That will get the weight off!" I began a detox program to take the weight off, thinking at the end of the two weeks, I would jump back on the health wagon and go on what is called a modified food diet. A modified Food diet was a diet devoid of wheat, gluten, sugar, and dairy for the remaining two weeks. I wanted to stop my sugar and carbohydrate cravings that seemed to take over my mind and my body.

Three days into the detox, I began to feel mentally exhausted and lethargic. Physically, it was as if everything hurt. I actually felt like I had the flu; however, I knew that I did not. It would have been so easy to give in at this point, as the struggle did not seem worth it. I decided to use far infrared heat therapy to help pull and rinse the remaining toxins from my body via the lymphatic system as my legs were swollen, felt like they weighed 100lbs each and hurt like the dickens!

After only two days, I began to feel stronger and reconnected with myself. I had a feeling of determination to succeed, I was ready to stand up and fight. According to Ambika Wauters, our root Chakra is developed between the ages of birth and seven years of age, and it is during this time of early development that imbalances within the root Chakra can happen and affect us for the rest of our lives. I find it interesting that I detoxed for seven days, then after seven days of detox, the emotions that governed my root Chakra seemed to be healthier and more balanced and alive!

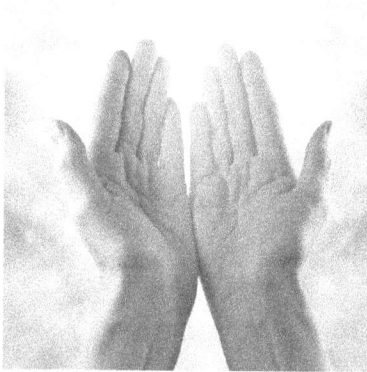

|Through the Magnifying Glass

In working with my clients and on my own personal issues, I found that holistic Chakra balancing therapy is most effective in clients who follow customized alternative therapies that address the underlying spiritual, mental, physical, and emotional issues occurring in the lower and higher levels of consciousness, where we find the subtle energy bodies.

Furthermore, a careful evaluation of events and memories during a client's seven-year life cycles may be helpful in pinpointing the underlying causes of Chakra imbalances. Since human experiences are unique and require different approaches for healing, by addressing unresolved issues and wounds during a particular seven-year life cycle, the Chakras can become more balanced. A combination of alternative therapies – in particular, color, crystal, aromatherapy, sound, hypnotherapy, and homeopathy – are implemented to accelerate healing, There is not one method that works for everyone, and oftentimes it takes several tries with various techniques to balance and restore the Chakras.

HOLISTIC CHAKRA BALANCING

Chakras are best balanced, starting with the root, and progressing upward toward the crown. An unstable root Chakra destabilizes the Chakras above it, so it is best to balance the root Chakra and continue working in an upward fashion through the Chakras. The three lower Chakras are the densest ones and must be cleared and balanced first, so that the above remaining Chakras can be cleared in the process. The lower Chakras deal with lower basal needs; therefore, feelings of stability, security, and love must be established first, before working in the higher spiritual levels of consciousness. This would also follow the principles of Abraham Maslow's Hierarchy of Needs, discussed in his 1943 paper, A Theory of Human Motivation. Maslow proposed a pyramid of needs; higher needs only coming into focus once the lower needs are met. The lower needs at the bottom of the pyramid include the basal needs such as breathing, sleeping, eating, basic psychological needs, safety, etc., while the top end of the pyramid focuses on self-actualization. The same is true for Chakra balancing; it is always best to work on

stabilizing the root Chakras and to move up through the higher Chakras.

Working with clients to balance their Chakras from the bottom up, I noticed the unbalanced upper Chakras became much easier, quicker, and lighter to restore and balance. Many of the basal worries had created imbalances, so by clearing the lower survival and security worries, the upper Chakras were able to come back into balance. Additionally, I was able to see that obstacles and barriers to success are deeply rooted. Like the layers of the onion, all the issues must be peeled back to reveal even deeper imbalances. Holistic Chakra balancing is most effective when treatment is carried out over an extended period of time (three to six months, or more) to uncover and release as many issues as possible. One Chakra affects the balance of the others, so it is important to follow through and not give up before the Chakras are completely cleared, restored, and balanced. The full process may take longer for some people than others, depending on the nature of the issues and how deeply rooted they are. The client cases shared in this book discuss those for which positive results were seen after three to six months of therapy; some up to a year. Once the Chakras were cleared, the problems did not return. Health was greatly improved on all levels: physical, emotional, mental, and spiritual.

Chakra balancing involves working with higher levels of consciousness and clearing not only what appears in the physical body, but also what remains unseen and unresolved in the subtle energy bodies. Western medicine only addresses the physical body and does not explore the imbalances in the subtle energy bodies. For this reason, Western medicine focuses on disease management, but never really gets to the underlying cause of problems, which may exist in unseen energy bodies. By clearing the Chakras, issues are resolved in the higher levels of consciousness, leading to a trickle-down effect of healing where the energies are restored and the physical body benefits from the energy correction.

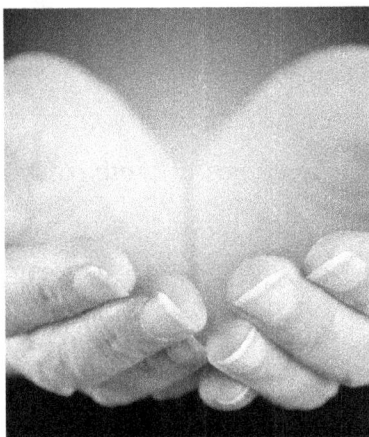

Has Western Medicine Failed Us?

No one can dispute the validity of Western medicine for acute conditions that require immediate attention. Fixing a broken leg, resuscitating the heart after a heart attack, or stitching a deep, open wound… all immediate issues that require acute medical care.

However, when it comes to chronic conditions, the Western model of disease management has failed to create a healthy society. Instead, it has created an unhealthy, codependent society that "lives with chronic conditions," rather than resolving and clearing them. Holistic Chakra balancing, which treats the body's subtle energy centers and resolves imbalances of mind, body, emotion, and spirit, is an effective alternative to resolving chronic conditions – and a much more comprehensive, successful approach that heals higher levels of consciousness in order to address physical, emotional, mental, and spiritual issues that manifest on the physical plane.

Western medicine is also based on an empirical method, which is the collection of a large amount of data to make a verifiable conclusion. Where, on the other hand, Chakra balancing involves an intuitive approach, since Chakras have not been confirmed scientifically. The lack of verifiable data should not deter us, as a society, from comparing the effectiveness of holistic Chakra balancing with the effectiveness of Western disease management to see which modality has a higher success rate, both in terms of improved health and lowered health care costs. Furthermore, it would be interesting to explore the long-term implications of integrating holistic Chakra balancing techniques with the traditional Western health care model. Would we be a healthier society if we started using holistic Chakra balancing in Western medicine?

The question might be addressed as to why there has not been sufficient study documentation to give the kind of empirical data validating the value of this practice. Would it be possible to get a grant, take a "Population" such as a prison, and gather sufficient data to provide validation for alternative healing methodologies and move forward to ensure a healthier society?

A Retrospective View

In following clients through their various challenges, I found that holistic Chakra balancing does have a positive effect on addressing and resolving chronic issues that are otherwise resistant to a "quick fix." Furthermore, I was able to recognize that working on the Chakras from "the bottom up" has an accelerated healing effect on each of the upper Chakras. As the root, sacral, and solar plexus are balanced, it then becomes easier to balance the heart, throat, brow (third eye), and Crown Chakras.

Holistic Chakra balancing can accelerate healing on all levels: body, mind, emotion, and spirit. A combination of holistic techniques is essential for Chakra balancing. Each person has unique life experiences and challenges require specific treatments. After balancing the Chakras, a maintenance program may be useful to maintain the proper energy balance in order to prevent the manifestation of physical ailments in the future.

For future study, it would be interesting to explore the long-term effects of Chakra balance maintenance throughout life, and the positive health implications of Chakra balance as a lifestyle choice. It would also be noteworthy to see if Chakra balancing therapy could increase life span, decrease disease rates, slow down the process of aging, and create a healthier, more balanced society. Taking it a step further, it would also be remarkable to evaluate the impact of Chakra balancing on global consciousness. As more and more people become balanced in their energy centers, would they create a balance for the entire planet resulting in less war, conflict, and strife, and a renewed sense of peace, prosperity, health, and abundance.

Awakening to the Universe

The intention behind helping you discover Holistic Chakra Balancing and the Power of Color Therapy is to impress upon you the correlation between the two. As noted throughout the book, the seven chakra centers control the energetic biological functions in the areas located throughout the body. Adding color therapy to chakra healing provides a more focused and direct modality for restoration. The chakras respond with more healing if the color being applied corresponds to their natural color and frequency. Although the body also responds to color, meditation, aromatherapy and music, the combination of chakra balancing and color therapy – acting as conduits for our body's life forces, will be a key player in the future of preventative medicine.

Chakras are known to be the spiraling vortexes of energy, which flow through the body and circles along the body's electrical pathways. On a physical level, each Chakra is inner-connected with our nerves, our senses and our glands. We find them to be where we allow the Universe to create our energy, reflect our consciousness and establish our awakening to the Universe.

Color therapy has long been a topic of interest in my life; it is performed in a variety of media. These media range from immersing the client in a room surrounded by a specific color that they need, to having the client ingest the essence of the healing color in digestible oils. As I progress through my work as a metaphysical practitioner, I am exposed to many different forms of thought and belief. Many of my clients practice varying healing techniques within the spiritual practices. In working with my clients and helping them to identify or remove obstacles in this life, I have heard accounts of many different ways that color has been used in healing. Within the multiple therapies that utilize color, I have even found variations of the color schematic in relation to the healing practices standard method (i.e., Sanskrit Chakra balancing). For example, one client who practices Chakra-balancing work on a daily basis draws upon colors for her Chakra system that deviate from Sanskrit practice and are, to my knowledge, not published as suggestions in any religious or healing texts.

As a result of my exposure to the wide array of ways in which color is used, along with my growing interest in color therapy, I believe it is important to further explore color as a healing tool and examine its effects on our subtle energy systems. How does color impact an energy body? How many levels of an etheric body does one specific color heal or affect in a positive way? Why is it that one energetic being intuitively knows to envision the use of golden light in her heart Chakra, while others call upon pink? What is the importance of a specific color for a client in removing his or her blocks?

It is my belief that the answers to these questions could profoundly impact the professional practice of metaphysics. The deeper our understanding of color and the energy system, the more opportunity we have to positively help our energetic clients with balance, life lessons, knowledge, health and prosperity.

SECTION II

The Healing Power of Color

Color is used in many different forms of healing techniques within, and outside of, this dimensional plane. In researching color and its effect on our energetic bodies, it is important to define ourselves as an energy system. It is also important to define our energy structure at the ethereal, aura and physical levels to better discuss the possible uses of color therapy to the energy system.

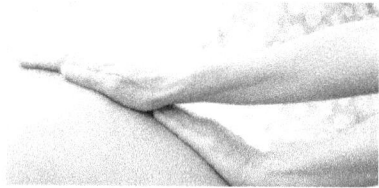

In researching material to offer a broad overview of color therapy, I consulted many written articles, books and other documentation. Enjoy this short prose of key information gathered from authors around the world, and resulting from their studies in the areas of the spirit/ethereal, physical and emotional body, the Chakra system and Color Therapies.

I specifically found interest in the six (or greater) levels of soul bodies as described by Meg Blackburn Losey, MSC.D., Ph.D. (2004). Losey theorizes that we exist on more than one level. She states, "We have many bodies that contribute to our experience on this plane. Those bodies, our etheric bodies, appear in a specific order, and each of these bodies has a particular function."

Our etheric bodies, in order, are: Physical, Emotional, Mental, Intuitive, Causal (more than one is possible) and Soul. Readied with this knowledge, we can better discuss the importance of understanding the impact of these etheric bodies and their relation, if any, to color.

Ambika Wauters (2002), author of "The Book of Chakras, Discover the hidden forces within you," provides a great description of the concepts and details of the seven primary Chakras. According to Wauters, "[the Chakras] are the body's energy centers through which the life force flows, helping you to maintain physical, mental, emotional and spiritual balance". Her writings contain great information pertaining to the Chakras and their relationship to the Physical, Emotional and

Mental bodies. In discussing the human energy system, Wauters writes, "The vital force of the human energy system directs energy through the layers of subtle energy bodies… The vital force exists in all life forms and is the same whether found in a human being, an animal or a plant. The force directs our physical energies, using the Chakras as conductors to filter energy through the physical body."

In her earlier writings, Wauters took an innovative approach, in which she wedded the Chakra system to Carl Jung's archetypes. Integrating the two powerful healing systems, she created an easier process for identifying emotional blocks and negative patterns. According to Wauters, "The archetypes that we live out reflect the psychological patterning of self-care and worthiness, demonstrating the degree to which we love and cherish ourselves. They are a clear manifestation of our emotional state and the stage we have reached in our growth and maturation."

Another book, integral to this writing is "Crystal, Color, and Chakra Healing" by authors Sue and Simon Lilly. Their writings about the details of the three forms of healing were easy to follow and inspired my message. In their writings the couple explains the use of working with crystals that are of the appropriate color needed to heal the client. According to the

Lilly's, there are two primary paradigms for using crystals in healing. The first one they describe is the Spiritual Paradigm, which is based on the belief that crystals are used to channel, direct and amplify energy from the healer, or the spiritual realms.

The second paradigm the authors discuss is the Resonance Placement Paradigm. This crystal-healing paradigm is based on the concept that "many different stones may be used, each one chosen for a particular beneficial effect on the client. Placed on or around the body, the color, shape and composition of the stones are thought to create a resonance that encourages healing to take place." It is the last paradigm that I draw upon for the purpose of this book, along with their detail in color therapy.

In discussing color therapy and its effects on the energy system, Joe Vitale (2005) connects energy, via the energy system, to everything we do in life. He has said, "Once you change the way you are inside, the outer world changes." I know this statement may seem contradictory to color therapy in the sense that in the professional practice of metaphysics, we think of color therapy as energy that is outside going inward. However, I believe his discussion of energy, which is specifically centered on changing our inner energy to attract what we desire, is a good example of the polar portion for how energy itself works within the energy system.

Lastly, in support of energy, the energy system and color therapy, Ann Wigmore (1983) declares, "An individual aura emanates from and surrounds each person. The aura is a force field of swirling frequencies in various colors that is readily and clearly perceivable to the clairvoyant... Rays from the human aura project from the physical, emotional and spiritual body..."

The Seven Chakras of Color

Color is universal. The world is full of color in a wide variety of hues and shades. The palette of primary colors changes, depending on which the circle of society – science, art or other – is defining the color spectrum. For the purpose of this document, "Color Therapy" references the seven colors that define wavelengths of visible light. These are: red, orange, yellow, green, blue, indigo, and violet. This set of colors is also primarily used in Chakra balancing work, where the color red represents the lowest Chakra point, and the color violet represents the highest.

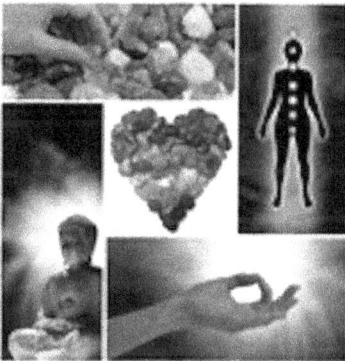

According to Sue and Simon Lilly (Crystal, Colour and Chakra healing, 2006), "Many of the pioneers of colour healing found that their clients benefited from drinking water charged with natural sunlight or specific wavelengths of colour. Some theorized that the atomic structure of the water was somehow altered and given particular life-enhancing properties." This information further inspires one to consider how color impacts an energetic body and how a combination of colors applied to different aspects or areas of the body can induce rapid and specific healing.

In discussing the findings of color therapy and its affects on a body's energy, it is important to remain familiar with the Chakra teachings. The more common Chakra teachings within the world are those known as the Sanskrit Chakra teachings. Many metaphysical websites and stores contain one or more visual aids that represent the Sanskrit Chakra colors as related to each of the major seven Chakras located around the physical body. In Sanskrit Chakra balancing, the primary seven Chakras from lower body to higher are: Root, Sacral, Solar Plexus, Heart, Throat, Third Eye and Crown. According to written texts about Sanskrit Chakra balancing, each of the seven primary Chakras operates best when the Chakra color is brought into balance with the Chakra itself, thus balancing the Chakra. In standard

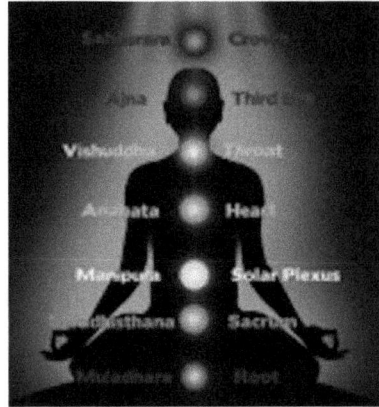

Chakra-balancing teachings, the individual should bring to balance his or her Chakras by calling forth the Chakra color that corresponds to the needed vortex of energy.

The Root Chakra

The Root Chakra is the lowest of the seven primary Chakras. It is appropriately named "Root," as its primary focus is to keep us "grounded" to the earth and physical plane. The Root Chakra is the vortex whereas an energetic body's main concern is "survival" and meeting the physical body's needs. A person with an unhealthy Root Chakra displays fear for his survival in this life and on this physical plane, while a person with a healthy, balanced Root Chakra is secure with his place on earth, has a high sense of self-assurance that he can provide for himself and is well grounded in relation to the events that surround his life. An out-of-balance Root Chakra can be balanced by "breathing in" the color red.

The Sacral Chakra

The second-lowest Chakra is the Sacral. This vortex is strongly associated with and linked to one's sexuality and one's emotional self. An unbalanced Sacral Chakra in often evident in a person who displays an extreme expression of emotions. That person may be strong and brash in his emotional display, or extremely reserved and quiet – either extreme could be reflective of one whose Sacral Chakra is out of balance. "Breathing in" the color orange to the Sacral Chakra can bring this vortex into balance.

The Solar Plexus Chakra

The next Chakra level up from the Sacral is the Solar Plexus. The Solar Plexus, according to Sanskrit teachings, is associated with an energy body's self-esteem and self-confidence. The Solar Plexus Chakra is associated with the color yellow, which when in balance, will bring balance to this vortex. An unhealthy Solar Plexus Chakra is characterized by insecurity, an excessive concern about what others think, and a constant need for reassurance from others. Bringing this Chakra into balance helps one to strengthen one's concept of self and one's self-confidence therein. This Chakra can help a person to feel his or her own personal power.

The Heart Chakra

The middle Chakra, the Heart Chakra, is cradled between the three lower Chakras and the three upper Chakras. An unhealthy or out-of-balance Heart Chakra can lead a person to feel unworthy of love, fear rejection or even to "love too much." It is no surprise that the primary areas of a person's life affected by this Chakra are love and relationships.

Meanwhile, a person with a healthy and balanced Heart Chakra will display characteristics such as: unconditional love, compassion and nurturing. Although non-Sanskrit practitioners may presume that this Chakra comes into balance when the color red is breathed in, it is actually brought into balance through the use of green or pink.

The Throat Chakra

Above the Heart Chakra is the Throat Chakra. The Throat Chakra, according to Sanskrit teachings, is all about self-expression and communication. An individual with a healthy Throat Chakra will display their optimum communication skills and techniques. They will not be afraid to communicate their needs nor to express their opinions to others. On the flip side of the coin, a blocked Throat Chakra would hinder communication (including listening to others) and self-expression, and might cause a person to interpret information in an overly critical way and to suppress self-expression via overly extreme self-discipline. The throat Chakra is linked to the color blue; some say the peaceful blue of Jesus breathed into this Chakra helps them to breath in peace; which allows people to better listen, speak and express themselves.

The Third Eye Chakra

The sixth Chakra is referred to as the Third Eye Chakra. This Chakra is about intuition and inner wisdom. According to Sue and Simon Lilly in their book "Crystal, Color, and Chakra healing" (2003), "The Chakra located in the centre of the forehead is called ajna, meaning 'to perceive and to command." Its job is to perceive and interrupt both the thoughts within oneself, and the world outside. An unhealthy Third Eye Chakra is often evident in a person who is too logical, arrogant, or undisciplined or who doesn't see the larger picture. A person who is highly intuitive or can see clearly the world that surrounds him most likely has a healthy and balanced Third Eye Chakra. In order to bring this Chakra into balance and its appropriate spinning speed, bring out the Indigo light.

The Crown Chakra

The last Chakra within the seven primary Chakras is referred to as the Crown Chakra. To properly balance and open this Chakra, call forth the violet light. This Chakra strengthens the spirituality and selflessness within an individual. An individual with a blocked Crown Chakra does not experience his spirituality and thus loses his sense of "belonging." Opening and keeping this Chakra balanced is not a destination, it is the journey to more personal enlightenment.

| A Study in Color

The Rebel

Through my work, I have met many interesting personalities. One such personality tends to call forth and visualizes colors in a different way than in the traditional Sanskrit formation. During my first encounter with this rather strong personality, whom I shall call Hailey, I was compelled to inquire why she deviated from documented practices. "Because Spirit guides me to," she candidly stated. That's all it took to clarify for me that with Spirit guiding her to call forth a different set of color energies into her subtle energy system and vortexes, Hailey must have been doing so because it satisfied some aspect of her needs in order to raise above her specific entities, health issues, or life challenges.

HOLISTIC CHAKRA BALANCING

A continually interesting study, I found one deviance from tradition is how Hailey visualized inhaling the green light of healing into her Solar Plexus Chakra, which is "intrinsically linked with our sense of self-worth and personal power" (Wauters, "Chakras and their Archetypes," 1997). The Solar Plexus acts as a gatekeeper to energy. It controls the "inhale" and "exhale" of energy created by our exchange with other energies. It is important to have a strong, well-balanced Solar Plexus Chakra, as it allows us to define who we are and keep clear boundaries for others, and ourself and be clear about how we expect to be treated.

The Sanskrit version of Chakra balancing identifies yellow as the appropriate color to "inhale" or call forth when balancing this Chakra. According to Lillian Vernon-Bonds ("Health Essentials: Colour healing," 2001), "Yellow is the brightest color in the spectrum. Its sunny hue brings clarity of thought, warmth and vitality. Yellow broadcasts a feeling of well being and self-confidence." In most of my research, I have found the characteristics of yellow to be similar to, or exactly described as, the solar plexus Chakra. Which leads me to question whether the definition of yellow for the purpose of Chakra balancing was simply derived from the Sanskrit Chakra for which the color is called forth.

The green vibration of light is often associated with healing and revitalization. However, it is also known to be a color of growth and transformation, as reflected in nature. In

believing that we are all one and that we are perfect beings, I believe Hailey's choice of green specifically aids her energy to grow in her sense of self and self-power. Although calling yellow to her Solar Plexus Chakra would not cause harm and would in fact allow Hailey's energy to rise in well-being and confidence, the green is simply a different choice, and it helps her energy to grow and bloom. The truly interesting fact regarding Hailey is her strong sense that "we" are here to learn… that life is about lessons, plain and simple. This belief greatly corresponds with calling in a "growth" color to her Solar Plexus Chakra (self-worth and personal power).

Expanding Hailey's personal and spiritual growth, as those relate to her use of green light with her Solar Plexus

HOLISTIC CHAKRA BALANCING

Chakra and energy aspects, she continues to show transformation within the various energetic aspects of herself. Those energetic aspects in order are: Physical, Emotional, Mental, Intuitive, Causal, (Meg Blackburn Losey, MSC.D., Ph.D., 2004).

Since Hailey began calling in the green light to her solar plexus and to the energetic bodies surrounding, and within, her physical body, many changes have occurred. The primary change noted by Hailey (prior to my work with her) is her ability to better outline and define her relationships with her family. Prior to calling in the green light, she tended to become involved in abusive, manipulative relationships which people who took advantage of her weaknesses. Now, Hailey has managed to set clear boundaries for her relationships, including severing the relationships she knew were just not healthy.

Although she does so less frequently than her daily balancing of Chakras, Hailey also calls on the green light to aid her in healing her higher aspects. In the past few years, I have noted that her emotional self has been undergoing a visible transformation. The "emotional body" is the etheric body closest to the physical body. Due to its closeness to the physical body, it is highly affected by our human experience and reflects emotional traumas, along with insecurities and emotional injury. According to Losey (Pyramids of Light, 2004), "The emotional body is the largest etheric contributor to our physical disorders and pain."

Calling upon the healing green light to her emotional body has allowed Hailey to shed past traumas and injuries through its revitalization aspects. With the releasing of her emotional pain, her insecurities have lessened and her sense of self-worth has increased. By specifically calling upon the color green, Hailey has transformed herself from an abused, wilted spirit into a woman who is less and less frequently looking into her past. She has been successful in creating relationship boundaries and redefining family relationships into relationships of healing and support. Hailey is more confident and better able to seek out her current life traumas and analyze them, even inquiring of family and friends about their viewpoints on events in family history and current events. Reaching (growing) out rather than wilting inwardly, Hailey has recently realized that only she is holding onto the trauma from those events.

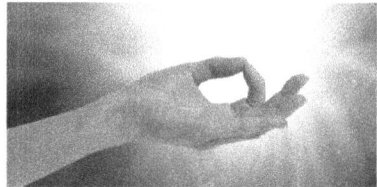

The color green has allowed her to grow in her self-confidence and to reach out and communicate with those past painful relationships. As a result this is allowing Hailey to heal the traumas of her childhood, which related to dramatic family incidents. Every week I saw her release those injuries and traumas like the layers of an onionskin, pioneering a transformation into a confident and secure woman.

I have been able to follow Hailey's use of green with her etheric aspects to one additional layer of her etheric self, her Mental Body. The "Mental body" is aptly named, as it is a body of thought, wisdom and knowledge. Those intuitives who are able to see different etheric bodies describe the Mental body as being yellow in color. As stated previously, Hailey calls forth energy to her Chakras, which are outside the Sanskrit teachings. She also draws on and absorbs those specific colors to all her etheric bodies and aspects.

At the time that I met Hailey, she was intently focused on her business. With complete faith and a perceived understanding of the powers of manifestation, she was working diligently to get her business up and running, with an intensity that could not be out-matched. Her knowledge and wisdom manifestation was "stuck" in material possession and physical manifestation. However, throughout the past few years, I observed her shift in the knowledge that happiness and joy (two items she recurrently stated she wanted) were not found in the material. Her business wasn't truly making her happy. Calling for the green light into her yellow mental body has transformed and grown Hailey's wisdom into the spiritual understanding that happiness and joy come in many different forms.

What does this mean to you? Simply to understand if you would like to have happiness and joy, you need to focus on manifesting the exact items you desire and allowing the happiness and joy to come in whatever form they arrive. Although Hailey still struggles with the allowing portion of manifestation (and thus needs to focus more on healing and growing her Solar Plexus Chakra), she has progressed and now displays behavior that indicates that her old patterns of thought on manifestation and happiness within this life are less complicated than she personally chooses to make it. Hailey's understanding and wisdom that she is blocking her "receipt" of the very manifestation she has created, allows her new "wisdom" to work through her physical mind and release those blocks of doubt, fear and impatience.

A Colorful Group

In one group study regarding color, the etheric bodies and the effects of color upon the subtle energy system, I instructed the group to attempt to wear outfits that were colors of the Sanskrit Chakra system chart. The case study required each participant to agree to record for a period of seven consecutive days a reflection of their thoughts and moods in relation to the color that they wore or by which they were dominantly surrounded. Each group member was therefore instructed to use their best attempts to either surround themselves in the colors of the Sanskrit Chakra methods or wear outfits that were dominantly those colors. It was requested that each client choose to begin at either the highest Chakra color (the Crown Chakra, violet), or at the lowest Chakra (the root Chakra, red) and wear colors sequentially down/up the Sanskrit chart. The study further requested that each client note the dominant color found in their wardrobe, home and work. Meanwhile, it was requested that the clients document their mood and thoughts throughout periods of the day – such as early morning, arrival at work, mid-day, afternoon and evening – while providing details about their surrounding colors.

Red

Interestingly, some commonalities began to emerge among the participants' observations. All of the clients had a

red item in their closets to wear. When wearing red, the majority noted common moods of strength and self-confidence rooted in their discussions with peers or leaders. They noticed that their peers listened to them attentively as they presented solutions or results to a group. The obvious results from wearing red reflect that the case study participants maintained a relatively health root Chakra and were able to reflect a self-mastery to their co-workers. They were presenting themselves as secure in their world and in their places within their organizations and among their peers.

Also interesting was the participants who observed those around them who wore red made note that their peers dressed in red seemed stronger or sturdier than others. They also noted that some, although not all, of those co-workers also seemed angry and ready to, "Charge at me or into the situation full force." I asked the group if they were willing to surround those who presented as "angry" in a pink light of love, from their heart Chakras, the next time that they themselves wore red. Of those who agreed, one participant came back and reported a subtle change in that being's presentation to him. "There was a definite 'calming' effect on the person, especially if I kept calling in the light through my Crown Chakra and sending out the pink light from my heart to theirs. It took about 5-10 minutes to noticeably see the person appear less angry with me."

Orange | Yellow | Gold

It was noted that three of the four clients found very little orange, yellow or gold within their closets. Of those clients who did have some form of those colors in their wardrobes, wearing the colors led to a state of agitation. This was especially found in clients who wore the orange or yellow following a 'red' day. These clients used descriptions such as "uncertain of myself," "worried about presenting to others," "felt unsafe and wanted to keep my thoughts and observations to myself," "I was inward and withheld from participating in group discussions to resolve company issues." Of all the

Chakra colors, these were the hardest for the clients to continue to wear and surround their energies within.

Three participants of the study admitted to immediately removing an article of clothing or jewelry that contained those colors, immediately upon arriving home. Interestingly, each of these participants "needed" to treat themselves to a personal indulgence that evening. One female client, whom we will call "Eileen," drew a bath for herself, utilizing the powerfully relaxing scent of lavender to ease her into a state of relaxation and comfort. Interestingly enough, violet is a color that assists beings in balancing their Crown Chakras. When your Crown Chakra is balanced, the subtle energy beings take responsibility for themselves. You will see your place in the world and understand it better. If you are uncomfortable in yellow, gold or orange, it indicates a possible imbalance in your energy field. The imbalance presents as self-doubt, insecurities of the self's place within a group, and a need for reassurance. In Eileen's attempt to call forth the essence of violet within her bath, it stands to reason that this being wanted to solidify her connection to the One, and to find her place in the universe and be assured of her position with it.

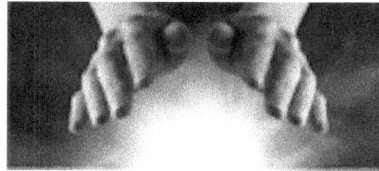

Although this method immediately soothed Eileen's physical and emotional state, the true reflection of this exercise for the participant is an imbalance in her Solar Plexus and Sacral Chakras. As such, we began working in different color therapy processes, including Feng Shui, to assist her energy into balance.

Green

Once group participants reached the color green, commonly worked with for the heart Chakra, it was noticed that color was also limited within the wardrobe. However, none of the case study participants noted any challenges in wearing or surrounding themselves with that color. For the most part, it was reported that the days were "relaxing and flowed well." "The day seemed filled with opportunities; I didn't really see any obstacles," reported one participant.

Green is a color of transformation and growth. For some, transformation and growth can be uncomfortable, believed to be an underlying belief of unworthiness or a misconception of having been betrayed by their peers. If you are an individual with a balanced heart Chakra who surrounds yourself with green, the day should appear to be filled with opportunities.

The subtle energy being would have feelings of compassion and nurturing. No matter what events surround you, the perception of that being would be one of positivity. Everything would be an opportunity to learn, grow, help a fellow person or nurture another to grow. Green is a powerful healing and transforming color.

Blue

During the study, the next color experienced by the group study was blue, for the throat Chakra – the next position up from the heart Chakra. I include the soft blue hue of Jesus' robe in the color therapy practice. This particular soft blue is a great hue in which to surround yourself when working on improving communications. It provides a feeling of peace and harmony with others. Not surprisingly, blue was one of the more common colors reflected in the study participants' wardrobes. This tranquil blue represents the quality of peace to many, and as such is near prophetic for the wearer and observer.

It isn't too surprising that no one in the study had difficulty wearing blue. I was intrigued, however, finding this the day most participants truly noted the colors of their surroundings and on their co-workers. In their peace and harmony, the study participants took more time noticing the attire of their co-workers and the reflections of that co-worker to themselves. Surrounding themselves in the soft hue of blue also generated a non-judgmental acceptance of their co-workers and surroundings.

Indigo

Indigo, a cross between the blue of the throat Chakra and the violet of the Crown Chakra created a challenge in being found in the wardrobes of the study participants. However, in true spirit of creativity, the participants chose to wear a little blue and violet, if no sole representation of indigo was to be found. The effects of this color varied among the study participants. Each had a slightly different reaction or understanding of how their day progressed within the indigo spectrum of the study. My conclusion is simple. Indigo is a color essence that helps the subtle energy force to bring to

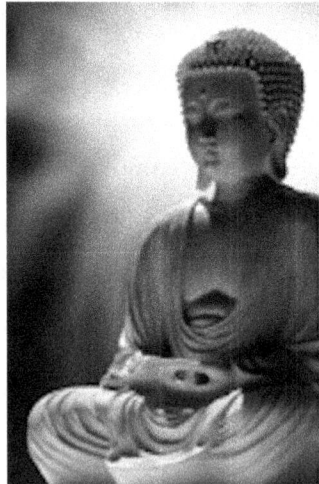

balance the third eye Chakra. In other words, each participant was bringing into balance that part of 'self ' that assists in being more intuitive and less attached to material things. You might find, then, in wearing indigo your being more attached to your higher intuition; your experiences more reflective of your personal needs as designated by your soul self. This "intuitive" color would reflect to the subtle energy life lessons that are being learned, or avoided.

In the analysis, such insight proved invaluable to the case study participants and to the future understanding of color therapists. One participant noted, "I feel like people are not being truthful or honest to me. I feel badly for thinking that they aren't being honest, but everything in my being tells me to put forth my best efforts and rise above office gossip." It was later discovered that this particular participant's company was outsourcing some sub-sections, or portions of a department, which held multi-functions within the organization. In listening to her intuitive wisdom to continue putting forth her best quality work, it is likely she unconsciously influenced decision-makers as they decided whether to let her go or to keep her within the department.

Violet

The top color on the Chakra spectrum is violet. Case study participants noted little effect in wearing this color. They were able to wear violet attire, or surround themselves with this color throughout the majority of the day, but noted very little reflection in regards to how they believed they were being affected by the color. Most participants did note a belief or feeling of self in relation to their surroundings. This day had very little agitation noted, except in dealing with individuals who were "too strongly rooted in their position" of an argument (specifically dominant in a red-hued wardrobe). "I kept thinking this guy would normally have me very frustrated by now [in how he was approaching the task at hand]; I really just sat back and didn't feel any need to interact with his energy. I felt safe and secure in knowing who I am and that I had a choice not to interact with his agitation [or] let it affect me. I didn't feel defensive and still held the belief that I could communicate my thoughts and ideas without confronting him."

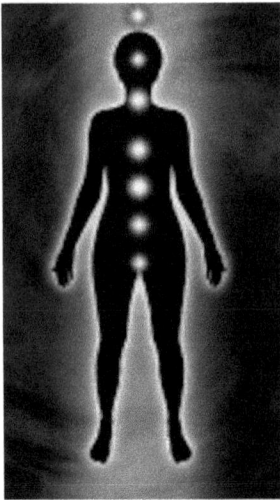

In that, while surrounding herself in violet, this client felt a sense of herself and her worth within the company. She was able to understand and allow her fellow employee his need to dominate and overrule, while understanding she had personal power in the form of choice. She had a sense of her place within the group and organization, which could have been amplified due to the violet attire and jewelry she was wearing.

The Effects of Color on Society

In today's modern world, scientists have documented the effects of color on society. The companies that are most color-influenced, according to the scientific studies, are retail establishments and the marketing community. Ask any

prominent marketer why they have chosen certain colors in the print ads or commercials of their clients, and they will inform you of the numerous studies indicating those colors generate improved sales. Orange, for example, has been scientifically noted to increase hunger in humans. As such, many establishments within the fast-food industry utilize the color in visible areas of their dining halls.

It should be no surprise to modern society, given its acceptance of notable color studies, that color affects our bodies. Color influences our choices, attitude and willingness to engage in activities. Professional metaphysicians who specialize in color therapy can greatly influence the transformation, growth and balance of a person's life. For example, teaching you about color and about how you are affected by color can help you to influence your choices and attitude in regard to how to flow more positively in your day. Once you understand how you react to or interact with specific colors, then you can generate a more conscious understanding of your co-workers, surroundings or your own response to the activities occur around you throughout that day.

Once metaphysicians better understand how color therapy influences modern society, corporations may also be able to help their employees experience more positive and productive days through the use of color on walls or in break rooms. Extending the concept of corporate America embracing color therapy within its walls, companies could hire color therapists as part of their Human Resources staffs. Trained and experienced color therapists could help the personnel flow of organizations and the interactions among personnel via recommendations of attire color, etc.

The concept of color therapists being hired on by American corporations is not exactly far-fetched. Major corporations already utilize tools once thought to be "metaphysical in nature." Common examples of these tools include handwriting analysis and behavior tests.

Since corporate America is a dominant figure in the American lifestyle, economy and daily life, one may conclude that color therapy should be utilized within those fortress walls. The subtle energy beings that are bombarded by negativity and stress each day may be able to rise above those agitations through the use of color. Should those employees be able to better flow with the daily routine of their corporate work requirements, the positive effects on those employees will filter into different aspects of their lives; including reductions in road rage and possibly violent crimes. Color therapy utilized en masse in daily life, can generate a positive outcome to our society. Embracing the subtle effects of color and color therapy could truly assist the world in becoming a brighter, more positive and peaceful place for daily living.

The Future of Color Therapy

It is my belief that color does affect our subtle energy systems on many levels including the physical, emotional, mental, intuitive, causal and soul, and could profoundly impact the professional practice of metaphysics. The deeper our understanding of individual color and the energy system, the more opportunity metaphysicians have to positively help our energetic clients remove blocks through customized color therapy.

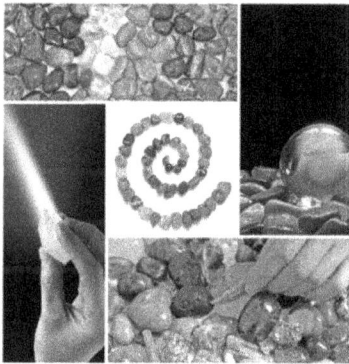

The clients gain a lifelong process for creating balance, addressing life lessons, acquiring knowledge and accepting health and prosperity in their lives. In the professional practice of metaphysics, we are all inter-connected and entwined; therefore, to be able to strongly impact other energetic beings in a positive way, impacts all life on earth in a positive flow

Section 1 Bibliography

Aromatherapy & Energy Chakras. Home. (2009 June 09)
http://thehealingmassage.com/aroma.aspx.

Brennan, Barbara. Hands of light: A guide to healing through
the human energy field. (1988). New York: Bantam
Books.

Burke, June K. (1998). Self discovery & manifestation.
Minneapolis: Burke-Srour Publications, Inc.

Centers for Medicare & Medicaid Services. (Retrieved 2014,
January 4).
http://www.cms.gov/Newsroom/MediaReleaseDatabase/P
ress-Releases/2013-Press-Releases-Items/2013-12-
17.html

Davis, Patricia. (2005). Aromatherapy: An A-Z: The most comprehensive guide to aromatherapy ever published. London: Vermilion.

Eden, Donna. (2008). Energy medicine (Revised). New York: Tarcher/Penguin.

Feinstein, David, and Donna Eden. (2008). Energy medicine balancing your body's energies for optimal health, joy, and vitality. New York: Tarcher.

Gardner-Gordon, Joy. (2005). Vibrational healing through the chakras with light, color, sound, crystals and aromatherapy. Berkeley, CA: Crossing Publications.

Goldman, Jonathan. (2008). The 7 secrets of sound healing. Carlsbad: Hay House.

Homeopathy. (2009). Answers.com - Online Dictionary, Encyclopedia and much more. http://www.answers.com/homeopathy.

Anodea, Judith. (2004). Chakra balancing kit: A guide to healing and awakening your energy Body. Riverside: Sounds True.

Anodea, Judith. (2004). Eastern body, western mind: psychology and the chakra system as a path to the self. New York: Celestial Arts.

Anodea, Judith. (1999). Wheels of life: A user's guide to the chakra system. St. Paul, Minn: Llewellyn Publications.

Klotsche, Charles.(1994). Color medicine: The secrets of color/vibrational healing. Sedona, Ariz. USA: Light Technology Publications.

Lansky, Amy L. (2003) Impossible cure: The promise of homeopathy. New York: R.L. Ranch Publications.

Leading Disease Management Organizations. (2008, Summer). Santa Cruz, CA: Health Industries Research Companies.

Lokhorst, Gert-Jan. (2009, June). Descartes and the pineal
    gland. Stanford Encyclopedia of Philosophy.
    http://plato.stanford.edu/archives/spr2009/entries/pineal-
    gland/.

Mercier, Patricia. (2000). Chakras balance your body's energy
    for health and harmony. New York: Godsfield P,
    Distributed by Sterling Publications.

Pond, David. (1999). Chakras for beginners: Honor your
    energy (For Beginners). Minneapolis: Llewellyn
    Publications.

Questions and answers about homeopathy [NCCAM
    Research Report]. (2009, June). National Center for
    Complementary and Alternative Medicine [NCCAM] -
    nccam.nih.gov Home Page.
    http://nccam.nih.gov/health/homeopathy/.

Sacred Centers (2009, June 03). Pathways for personal and
    global transformation - chakras, videos, workshops and
    books by Anodea, Judith. http://www.sacredcenters.com/.

Schnaubelt, Kurt. (1998). Advanced aromatherapy: The science of essential oil therapy. Rochester, VT: Healing Arts Publications.

Simpson, Liz. (1999). Book of Chakra Healing. New York: Sterling.

Wauters, Ambika. (2009, June 04) Spiritual homeopathy: Healing the subtle bodies of the human energy system. http://www.ambikawauters.com/journals/healingbodies.html

Wauters, Ambika. (1999). Life changes with the energy of the chakras. Freedom, CA: Crossing Publications.

Wauters, Ambika. (2002). The book of chakras: Discover the hidden forces within you. Danbury: Barron's Educational Series.

Wauters, Ambika. (2007). The Homeopathy bible: The definitive guide to remedies. New York: Sterling.

Zukav, Gary. (1990). Seat of the soul. New York, NY: Simon
& Schuster.

Section 2 Bibliography

Blackburn Losey, Meg. (2004). Pyramids of light.
Andersonville, TN, Spirit Light Resources.

Lilly, Sue and Simon. (2003). Crystal, color and chakra
healing. How to harness the transforming powers of color,
crystals and your body's own subtle energies to increase
health and well being. Blackfriars Road, London, Hermes
House.

Verner-Bonds, Lilian. (2001). Health essentials: Colour
healing – harnessing the therapeutic power of the rainbow
for health and well-being. Blackfriars Road, London,
Hermes House.

Vitale, Joe. (2007). Hypnotic writing: How to seduce and
persuade customers with your words. Hoboken, New
Jersey, John Wiley & Sons.

Wauters, Ambika. (1989) [Journey of self discovery] Chakras
and their archetypes: Uniting energy awareness and
spiritual growth. Berkley, California, The Crossing Press.

Wigmore, Ann. (1983). The healing power within. Wayne,
New Jersey, Avery Publishing Group INC

Wauters, Ambika. (2002). The book of chakras: Discover the
hidden forces within you. Hauppauge, New York,
Barrons' Educational Series, Inc.

SECTION III

Balancing Your Chakras Questionnaire

Read each phrase below, and if it describes you, mark the yes column. If the phrase does not describe you, mark the no column.

<u>YES NO</u> **ROOT**

I am a patient person.

I create a life that supports my being the best I can be.

I feel my life is stable at the moment.

I feel secure about my life.

I am grateful

<u>YES NO</u> **SACRAL**

I honor my body's needs for food, fluids, supplements, and sleep.

I deserve peace, beauty, and tranquility in my life.

I see the joy and pleasure in small things.

If I had less in my life, I would still feel abundant.

YES NO **SOLAR PLEXUS**

I value myself.

I respect myself for having done a good job at certain things in my life.

I am confident in my ability to do something well.

I am clear about the need to balance my personal power with humility and compassion.

I believe that freedom of choice is essential to my human development.

YES NO **HEART**

I find joy with people, nature and animals.

I feel love for others and myself in my life.

I create peace in my life.

I recognize that everyone is connected to me and we are all one at the core.

YES NO **THROAT**

I express my feelings with ease.

I offer my full support to others.

I honor my personal truth.

I enjoy being creative and it makes me feel good about who I am.

YES NO **THIRD EYE**

I respect the wisdom that comes from the life experience of my friends and elders.

I trust my ability in discerning good from bad.

I value knowledge that can make my life more meaningful.

I visualize what my life will be like in the future, whether it is one year, five years, or 10 years.

I trust my intuition.

YES NO **CROWN**

I have a spiritual context for holding the difficult and challenging experiences in my life.

I see the beauty in others.

I can feel blissful, even if all of my problems are not solved.

How Things Work:
Homeopathic Remedies

Homeopathic Color Therapy:

RED: This color promotes grounding. It anchors the spirit in the physical body. It can, however, create anger and aggression if used too often or too high a potency. This color helps with issues of constipation, problems of mobility and coordination. The only cautionary advice is to be careful not to inflame the emotions by constant repetition. Do not give red to an angry child.

ORANGE: This color gives vitality and energy. It stimulates the body towards activity and the emotions towards happiness. When given in conjunction with pink gives joy. Do not give this in the evening as it stimulates the system and can impede sleep.

YELLOW: This color works on the digestion and helps tone the digestive organs. It has been used to support assimilation and detoxification. At the emotional level it builds self-confidence and inner strength. This is a good remedy for children with ASD and DD.

GREEN: This color works to soothe the energy system. It increases the release of fluid in the body and is good for all forms of fluid retention. It calms the nerves, promotes relaxation. It can be given day or night.

PINK: is the color of mother love. It gives a sense of love and of being loveable. It is wonderful when nerves are frayed and parents or child are unhappy. It is used with orange to promote joy and with violet to help sleep.

TURQOISE: This color helps with self-expression. It stimulates the will function and aids in communication. It helps with sore throats, toothache and problems in the throat.

INDIGO BLUE: This color works to calm the mind. It stimulates thinking and aids cognitive abilities. It creates a level of detachment when the emotions are inflamed and engaged. Indigo helps the mind focus.

VIOLET: This color, along with pink, creates serenity, love and beauty. This is good for sleep insomnia.

MAGENTA: This color helps to develop insight and creativity. It can be used in place of red from grounding. This color aids creative expression and supports understanding.

SPECTRUM: A color to be used for chronic low energy, fatigue or exhaustion. It should not be used at night.

Homeopathic Sound Remedies

Middle C: promotes grounding, connection and engagement.

Note of D: This energizes and gives a deep sense of happiness and well being.

Note of E: This stabilizes a sense of self internally.

Note: F: This works on the heart forces and provides peace.

Note B: This works to foster emotional self expression.

Note A: this creates clarity of mind, and stable emotions.

High C: this creates a spiritual framework that unites the spirit with the physical body.

The Chord: This is a mixture of all notes and works to strengthen the Self.

Resourced: Ambika Wauters
http://www.lifeenergymedicine.com/journals/DDR.html

Breathing in the Rainbow

It is easy to heighten your well-being, through a simple breathing exercise that encourages your awareness of the seven primary chakra colors. The following simple steps will guide you through the process.

Feet slightly apart, arms by you side, and palms turned to the front... relax your shoulders and concentrate on your breathing.

Breathe deeply in through your nose, hold it for a few moment, and then breath out through your mouth as you relax from head to toes.

When you are exhaling... imagine that all the stress, toxins, and other negativity is leaving your body.

Concentrate on your favorite affirmations, to keep your mind from slipping off elsewhere! For example... if you are seeking to be more courageous, you would draw on the power of the color of red and voice or hold tightly in your positively affirmed thoughts, something of this nature: "I use the energy of the color red to provide courage and strength throughout." Or perhaps, "I am courageous and strengthened through the energy received from the color red." The two primary considerations are that the affirmation and the color matches the transformation you desire.

Make an affirmation to suit your situation, as you breath in and experience the colour filling your body.

Remaining open to the experience of color filling your body, allow it to travel up through your body, flowing from the top of your head, and returning once more to the earth.

Understanding the powerful energies of other colors, as may be applicable, repeat the process for each are of transformation you want. The colors of the earth will be returned to the earth; those of the sky will be returned there.

Complete your exercise by visioning yourself with the pure white light we know provides us protection. Completing the exercise on a daily basis, not only will you increase your awareness of each of the chakra colors, you will gain the benefit the healing properties we know are derived through color.

www.ingramcontent.com/pod-product-compliance
Lightning Source LLC
Chambersburg PA
CBHW071055040426
42443CB00013B/3339